The Battle of Shiloh

A Captivating Guide to the One of the Bloodiest Battles of the American Civil War

Free Bonus from Captivating History
(Available for a Limited time)

Hi History Lovers!

Now you have a chance to join our exclusive history list so you can get your first history ebook for free as well as discounts and a potential to get more history books for free! Simply visit the link below to join.

Captivatinghistory.com/ebook

Also, make sure to follow us on Facebook, Twitter and Youtube by searching for Captivating History.

Contents

Introduction

On April 6th and 7th, 1862, the armies of the Union and the Confederacy clashed near the small Methodist church called Shiloh in southeastern Tennessee along the Tennessee River. The word "Shiloh" means "place of peace" in Hebrew, but for many Americans at the time and since, the word took on a new meaning, for the Battle of Shiloh was the bloodiest battle fought on the North American continent at that time, and it remained near the top of the list of deadliest battles when the war ended in 1865.

Illustration 1: Re-creation of the original Shiloh church on the exact spot where it stood in 1862. The battle raged in and around the church at one point during the conflict. Courtesy Matthew Gaskill.

After 1865 and until relatively recently, the Battle of Shiloh was relegated to the back pages of history books, except among historians and Civil War buffs. The battles that took place in the eastern part of the country in the area around the capitals of the Union and the Confederacy (Washington, D.C, and Richmond, Virginia, respectively) were the focus of most of their attention. The stunning Federal (also referred to in the text as the Union, the Yankees, or the USA) defeat at the First Battle of Bull Run (also known in the South as the First Battle of Manassas), the drama between President Abraham Lincoln and General George McClellan, "Stonewall" Jackson's dashing Shenandoah Campaign, the talented general Robert E. Lee, the Battle of Gettysburg, and much else have always overshadowed the events in the Western theater of the Civil War.

However, it has been argued in more recent times that the battles in the Western theater and along the Mississippi River played a more decisive role in the defeat of the Confederacy (also referred to in the text as the CSA or the Rebels) than was previously believed, and it may have been the more important theater, as the Union cut key supply lines, drove deep into Confederate territory, seized or destroyed vital farming and industrial areas and ports, and eventually allowed General William Tecumseh Sherman to march to the Atlantic and threaten the rear of the bulk of the Confederate forces that were fighting in Virginia. For most of the war, the struggle in the East was mostly confined to Virginia, a small part of Maryland, and a town in Pennsylvania called Gettysburg. The Civil War in the West was fought over hundreds and eventually thousands of miles.

However, for the men that fought there and for the nation at large, the Battle of Shiloh was an absolute shock. It was the bloodiest battle of the war up to that time, and it saw more dead and wounded than the French and Indian War, the American Revolution, and the War of 1812 combined. It is no exaggeration to say that the news of Shiloh hit the people in both the North and the South in the same way as Pearl Harbor did decades later or even 9/11, which took place more than a century later.

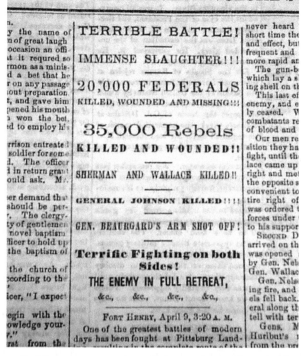

Illustration 2: Newspaper printed three days after the battle. In the confusion, rumors ran rampant. On the Union side, General Sherman was wounded, and General Wallace was killed. For the South, General Johnston (unlike in the newspaper article, it should be spelled with a "t") was killed, and General Beauregard was unscathed, while another CSA officer lost his arm.

Chapter 1 – Before the Battle

The Civil War began just shy of a year before the Battle of Shiloh. On April 13th, 1861, the Union fortress of Fort Sumter off the coast of Charleston, South Carolina, surrendered to the Confederate forces, which had been bombarding it for a day and a half. In command of the rebel guns pounding the fort was General Pierre Gustave Toutant Beauregard, a Louisianan and graduate of the West Point class of 1838, who excelled in the use of artillery. Beauregard (who is usually referred to by his initials, "P. G. T.," though he himself signed his letters as "G. T. Beauregard") would play a key role at Shiloh a year later.

Illustration 3: General Beauregard in 1862, about the time of Shiloh. Courtesy National Archives.

When reading histories of the Civil War and its battles, it's astounding how many times the word "shocked" is used to describe the reaction of both soldiers and civilians to an event, but in many ways, the American Civil War was the first "total war" in the modern sense. War was waged not only on the battlefield but also against civilians in cities, industries, agriculture, transportation, and, perhaps most of all, on the people's way of life and culture—that being slavery and the culture that supported it.

To us in the 21st century, the shock of the Southerners when their cities were bombarded and their slaves set free seems naive, but one must remember that, at the time, most wars were fought on isolated battlefields and that most of the casualties were the soldiers fighting on them. The carnage of the Civil War would largely remain on the battlefields, but many people, both within the country and overseas, were shocked by the amount of carnage they personally witnessed.

The Civil War was also the first war that was photographed to any large degree. While the camera technology of the day made it nearly impossible to capture battles as they happened, it was certainly able to take pictures of the dead, dying, and wounded. These photographs were also able to be seen almost immediately after the event, being displayed in newspapers, books, and exhibitions of the day, and the telegraph brought news of events on the battlefield almost as they happened. War was brought to people's front step during the Civil War, both figuratively and literally.

For about a decade before the war began, people all over the nation anticipated some sort of violent struggle between the North and South. While they did get a taste of the viciousness that could happen with the so-called "Border Wars" in Kansas and Missouri over the issue of slavery, virtually no one anticipated a nationwide conflict that would claim well over half a million lives.

It all started with Fort Sumter. The shock at the siege of Sumter was not at its casualty rate, as there were virtually none. No, the people of the country were shocked that the war, which had been brewing for some time, had actually begun. In the North, the shock was doubled by the fact that Sumter was a Confederate victory.

Three months after Fort Sumter, the armies of the North and the South clashed near the Bull Run creek near Manassas, Virginia, just some thirty miles south of Washington, D.C. The people, common soldiers, politicians, and many of the officers of both armies believed that once the "other side" got a taste of their "fighting spirit" and strength, the war would likely come to a rapid end.

Famously, people from Washington took trains and coaches out to the battlefield, where the armies, which were small at this point in the war, were massing, to watch the Rebels be defeated and then come to their senses and surrender. Instead, they saw the Federal troops defeated and had to join them in a panicked rout back to Washington.

Those in the South rejoiced over their victory, but they realized a number of things: they weren't strong enough to assault Washington, their soldiers and officers needed much more training, and that the war was not going to end any time soon.

A couple of smaller battles had been fought before Bull Run; their casualties numbered in the double digits. At Bull Run, just under five thousand men were killed or wounded. At Hatteras Inlet, after the First Battle of Bull Run, there were just over seven hundred casualties. At Ball's Bluff, Virginia, there were just over one thousand casualties. At Belmont, Missouri, there were nearly 1,500. At Mill Springs, Tennessee, there were 671. Forts Henry and Donelson in Tennessee saw a combined total of 17,517 casualties, the vast majority of which were Confederate prisoners. Wounded men accounted for most of the figures in the other casualties listed above. The total number for these battles was 26,195 men killed, wounded, missing, or taken prisoner.

By the time of Shiloh, many people had started to understand that the war was going to last much longer than they had initially believed but perhaps not *much* longer. And although the war had been bloodier than expected, people understood that, for the lack of a better phrase, "war is war."

The Strategic, Political, and Military Situation before Shiloh

The main Union Army in the East before Bull Run was commanded by Ohio General Irvin McDowell. His complete defeat at the hands of General P. G. T Beauregard led to his dismissal and the appointment of General George B. McClellan, who, like many of the higher-ranked officers of the Civil War, had fought in the Mexican-American War (and, in McClellan's case, with distinction). McClellan's skill in organizing the Department of the Ohio and his leadership of a small contingent of troops at the victory at Philippi (in what was to become West Virginia in 1863) on June 3rd, 1861, led to both rapid fame, as Philippi was the first land battle of the war, and rapid advancement.

McClellan was appointed the commander of the Military Division of the Potomac, meaning he was in charge of all Union troops in the Washington area. In August, this became the Army of the Potomac. McClellan was in command of the largest Union force, and he was second in military authority only to the famed hero of both the War of 1812 and the Mexican-American War, General Winfield Scott.

McClellan, even before the Civil War, had a reputation in the army as an excellent organizer and trainer of men. He also possessed a tremendous ego ("tremendous" might be an understatement), which only grew larger with the victory at Philippi, the adoration of the people of Washington, who greeted him as some sort of savior, and his appointment to command the largest section of the Federal army. His favorite nickname, which he encouraged but scarcely earned, was the "Young Napoleon." His troops also knew him fondly as "Little Mac," for he stood at about 5'8", which was actually just short of average at the time.

McClellan was indeed a great organizer and trainer of officers and men. Throughout his time in command, his troops seemingly adored him. He kept them well clothed, well fed, and, most glaringly, out of harm's way when Lincoln and others pressed him to lead his troops against the Rebels.

In the war's beginning stages, General Scott and his staff formulated a plan to subdue the Confederacy, which they dubbed the Anaconda Plan. Federal forces, which were greater in number on land and sea than the South, would pressure and attack the Rebels at all points: in the east near Richmond, down the vital Mississippi River, and all along the coast of the Confederacy, limiting transport and supply. They would squeeze the rebellion to death like an anaconda.

McClellan disagreed with this plan, but until Scott's resignation, which happened due to his ill health and being pushed aside by Lincoln in favor of younger officers (like McClellan), he was unable to do anything about it. However, when Scott retired, McClellan was put in overall command of the Union armies, so he was able to formulate the strategy he believed would win the war. This would be a grand plan in the style of Napoleon, which aimed at defeating the Confederacy in one overpowering campaign.

This campaign, known as the Peninsula Campaign, called for the landing of a massive Federal army behind the main lines of the Confederate Army in Virginia, south of Richmond. This Federal army would swiftly move up the James River Peninsula, seize Richmond, defeat the Rebel army, and end the war.

In many ways, the plan was innovative, but it was also impractical. The movement of so many troops down the Virginia coast would surprise no one (especially with the many Rebel spies in Washington), and the James River Peninsula was a relatively narrow piece of land that would allow a smaller force to hold back a larger one since the larger one would be unable to maneuver.

On top of all that, McClellan, for all his skill in training and supplying his men, turned out to be *extremely* cautious. Historians have debated the reasons for this, but many have landed on the opinion that his caution was due to his fear of losing his reputation. Once he arrived on the peninsula, McClellan began making incessant demands for more men, falsely believing that the Confederate force opposing him was at least as big if not bigger than his own 105,000 men and his many guns. For most of the campaign, the Rebel force was outnumbered by McClellan's forces, and had he been more decisive, he may have actually drove "onto Richmond!" (as the Union battle cry went). However, his delays and slow movement allowed the Confederates under General Joseph E. Johnston to reinforce and dig in. In the end, the Peninsula Campaign saw a series of hard-fought battles, some of which were won by the Union, but the U.S. forces never came close to Richmond.

After the Peninsula Campaign, which lasted from March through July of 1862, McClellan was relieved of his command of all Union armies, but he was left in command of the Army of the Potomac. His hatred for Abraham Lincoln, whom he vilified as a military "amateur" pushing him into battle before he was ready, only grew. For his part, Lincoln began to look for a replacement for McClellan, which he found in 1863 after McClellan's failure to pursue Robert E. Lee after the bloody Battle of Antietam on September 17th, 1862.

McClellan's successors as commander of the Army of the Potomac were Generals Ambrose Burnside, Joseph Hooker, and George Meade, respectively. Each of them had their chance to lead the Union to victory. Meade came close, winning the Battle of Gettysburg in July 1863, but he did not pursue and destroy Lee as Lincoln urged. He was replaced in the spring of 1864 by Ulysses S. Grant—the victor of Shiloh.

Chapter 2 – The Men and Their Weapons

The average age of the Civil War soldier was just under twenty-six years old, which is older than the bulk of the soldiers today. Most of them, especially those from rural areas and those from the South, had never been more than fifty miles from their homes if that. For this and other reasons, even in the North, most soldiers referred to themselves as residents of their state rather than calling themselves an "American." It was only sometime after the war was over that people began referring to themselves as Americans.

Most of the men had been farmers before the war, even though the urban population was beginning to grow by the start of the conflict. Within the Union ranks, some three hundred different trades/careers are listed, such as carpenter, surveyor, teacher, locksmith, mason, machinist, blacksmith, shoemaker, and teamster (those who drove wagons or transported goods). A number of them were lawyers or dentists, and some common soldiers were even local politicians or ministers (state and county politicians often secured an officer's commission for themselves, whether they had experience on the battlefield or not). The vast majority of soldiers were used to leading hard lives and fending for themselves. Aside from drills, uniforms, following orders, and, of course, getting shot at, army life could be much easier than relying on oneself for an income, and the fact that most soldiers had experience working with their hands helped too.

By the end of the war, about 25 percent (about 500,000 of 2 million) of the men in the Union Army were immigrants. That figure was less in the Confederacy, which was perhaps around 10 to 15 percent. The immigrants in the Union Army came from all over Europe (Europe was from where most immigrants came until well into the 20th century). The same held true in the Confederate Army, though it had a higher proportion of Irish and English immigrants within its ranks.

Hundreds of thousands of black Americans flocked to the Union banner to fight for the freedom of their fellows and, many times, family members in the South. Until the latter part of the war, blacks were limited to non-combat roles as laborers, which included the awful task of recovering bodies from the battlefield and burying them. The contingent of black Americans in the Union Army in Tennessee at the time of Shiloh held such roles. Of course, the enslaved blacks of the South were forced to work as laborers for the Confederate Army and as servants for many of its officers.

The uniforms of both sides varied, though there was more "uniformity" in the ranks of the better-equipped Union Army than there was in the Confederacy. Men from the North wore Union blue uniforms and a variety of hat styles, while the Rebels wore a patchwork (sometimes literally) of clothing. By the mid-point of the war, most Southern troops were wearing either the famous gray or perhaps the equally numerous yellowish "butternut" uniforms, with their own style of hat, although both sides began to wear the famous "kepi" by the end of the conflict. In April of 1862, the weather in western Tennessee was mild, but it was made worse by the fact that virtually all the uniforms were made of hot, slow-drying, heavy wool.

The Rebels frequently wore their own shirts and shoes (if they even had them) on the battlefield, and tragically, a number of Southern units still wore their state militia uniforms, which, unfortunately, were blue. On the Shiloh battlefield, perhaps hundreds of Rebel soldiers were wounded and sometimes killed by their own side, as they mistook them for the enemy.

What the average soldier carried with them depended on which army they were in. Generally speaking, Union soldiers were better equipped than their Confederate counterparts.

The typical Union foot soldier wore a belt from which hung a bayonet scabbard, a cartridge box, and a cap box ("caps" were the eraser-sized percussion charges that set off the gunpowder within the rifle). The cartridge box would hold about forty cartridges, which, for most of the war for most men, were paper tubes surrounding a Minié ball and black powder. (A Minié ball was actually a bullet-shaped lead projectile about half an inch wide and an inch or so long; the name came from its French inventor.) The cartridge box was usually lined with tin to help keep the contents organized. Each cartridge box had a pocket or pouch for a cleaning kit. Union soldiers carried anywhere between sixty and eighty rounds of ammunition.

Illustration 4: Modern replica of a Minié ball. Note the size.

Cavalry and artillerymen had less equipment for both mobility and necessity. In the fight at Shiloh, the cavalry played a smaller role than in some of the larger battles to come.

Unlike the Rebel soldiers, who generally carried their belongings in a cloth bag or tied-up blanket (unless they could get their hands on Union equipment), the men in blue carried a cotton or canvas knapsack that was most often painted black in order to stiffen and waterproof it. A blanket or shelter-half (half of a pup tent—the other half was carried by a comrade) was strapped to the top of the knapsack. At times, overcoats were also carried on the top of the knapsack. Additionally, a canvas bag or haversack was worn over the shoulder in which a soldier would carry food, personal items, coffee, and extra ammunition, among other items. These were also often painted to help keep the contents dry, and they contained a removable liner, for, after a time, the sack would begin to smell from the bacon, coffee, and tobacco carried within. Rebel soldiers grabbed Union haversacks whenever they could.

Every soldier carried a canteen. Early canteens were made of two pieces of tin with a pewter spout and a cork stopper. Most canteens were carried or were encased in a cotton or wool cloth, which would keep water cool and helped to prevent noise. Union canteens were also prized by Rebel soldiers, but early in the war, the canteens on both sides were notoriously flimsy.

Soldiers carried a knife, spoon, and maybe a fork, as well as a tin cup and perhaps a small frying pan or canteen half for cooking. Issued rations were most often salt pork or bacon and hardtack, a hard, dry biscuit or cracker that could last ages and tasted like it.

A wide variety of weapons were used during the Civil War. Like almost everything else, the industrialized North produced more and better weapons, with the possible exception of larger cannons, than the South. For a surprisingly long time, the men in gray used their own personal weapons brought from home. At Shiloh, most Rebel troops had never seen combat and were not able to be properly equipped. A great many carried shotguns or even old flintlocks from the Revolutionary War period. A handful even showed up with pikes or farming scythes.

However, most men at Shiloh, whether they were from the North or the South, carried the same or similar equipment as their comrades in other theaters of the war. Until close to the war's end, most men carried a muzzle-loading rifled musket. The advent of rifling (etching spiral grooves inside the barrel) meant both increased range and accuracy.

For those of you wondering why Civil War units lined up in rows and often fired at each other in standing positions, here are the answers. Firstly, until the advent of rifling, musket barrels were smoothbore, meaning it was just a simple tube. This meant limited range and limited accuracy, especially when you consider that many smoothbore weapons were made individually, not from prefabricated molds. To increase the effectiveness of these weapons, men were massed together. Within one hundred yards or so, this "wall of lead" was bound to hit something, at least most of the time.

However, with the advent of rifled barrels, which oftentimes came with sights, the effective range of these weapons increased manyfold. An average shot could hit a man-sized target with reliability at about three hundred yards away or even more. Sharpshooters might even hit something seven hundred to eight hundred yards away. This made the massing of the troops into the tight formations we see in Civil War books, movies, and re-creations a deadly error, and this tactic accounted for the high casualties at Shiloh.

An average soldier might load, fire, and reload his muzzle-loading weapon two or three times a minute. During the war, the self-contained bullet, with its own metal casing, powder charge, and projectile, was developed. Rifles now increasingly loaded at the breech, near the hammer. Even single-shot breech-loading weapons were faster than muzzle-loaders. Within a short time, rifles and carbines (a shorter barreled variant) began holding a number of rounds within them, making rapid fire possible. The famed Winchester rifle of the Old West was modeled on the Civil War-era Henry repeating rifle, which could hold sixteen rounds—fifteen in the tubular magazine that was under the barrel and one in the chamber, which was exceedingly dangerous since the weapon had no safety mechanism. To make things worse, dropping the weapon or jolting the hammer might cause a dangerous misfire.

Officers, cavalrymen, and some artillery soldiers carried pistols, which also came in a wide variety, some of which were actually variations of muzzle-loaders. Toward the end of the war, many of the pistols were quite similar to modern revolvers but oftentimes fired a larger caliber, making them quite deadly at close range.

The size and slow-velocity of Minié and round musket balls meant that, very often, wounds above the elbows or knees were fatal, and they usually blew a large hole open upon exiting the body.

Even deadlier was the artillery of the Civil War. At Shiloh, guns ranged from quite large 24-pound siege guns (named for the weight of the ammunition) to smaller 3- and 5-pounders. The armies of the Civil War also used mortars, which had a high trajectory, making them ideal for siege work (dropping shells over high walls), but very few if any mortars were used at Shiloh. These weapons bore little resemblance to modern mortars, as they were short, thick, and made of solid iron.

The cannons that were used at Shiloh and elsewhere during the Civil War fired a variety of ammunition. There was solid-shot, which is exactly what you think—a solid iron ball. There were explosive shells, hollow iron balls filled with black powder with a fuse that was cut to lengths depending on range. Spherical case-shot was similar to explosive shells, except they were filled with iron balls that would disperse upon explosion. Canister-shot was essentially a giant shotgun shell filled with iron balls, nails, scrap metal, or even rocks. Canister was used for close-range work, up to 250 yards. Double canister is just as you might imagine: two canister shells loaded at once. At Shiloh and other battles, canister was used to stop charges and break up formations.

Illustration 5: Civil War canister shell and contents.

Illustration 6: 24-pounder Union guns at Shiloh just days after the battle.

If you've seen any movies about the Civil War, one of the most ubiquitous scenes is that of the army field hospital with its bone saws, screaming, bloody bandages, and piles of amputated arms and legs. Actually, it was at Shiloh that the first designated field hospital was located. It was a canvas tent with open sides and a couple of tables. It was not until after Shiloh and its horrible casualties that work began on developing a functional medical corps and hospital system. Until then, medical assistance took place wherever surgeons (or what passed for them) happened to be. Frequently, these were local homes. This occurred at Shiloh, and makeshift hospitals were set up on the Union steamboats that brought reinforcements down and across the Tennessee River.

Illustration 7: Confederate artillery around the time of Shiloh.

Illustration 8: Shiloh veterans of the 7th Illinois in 1864. Their unit flag has "Pittsburg Landing" (another name for the Battle of Shiloh) and "Corinth" (which immediately followed Shiloh) sewn into it. Some hold newly issued Henry rifles.

Chapter 3 – Officers

Major General Ulysses S. Grant was the commander of the Army of the Tennessee at Shiloh, and he was also in overall command of the battle for the Union. At this stage of the war, Grant was a rising star, despite rumors of his heavy drinking. He had just won the Battles of Fort Henry and Fort Donelson on the Cumberland River northwest of Nashville, which allowed the Union to subdue those key Confederate strong points and protect the river traffic in northern Tennessee/southern Kentucky at a relatively low cost of Union lives. As a result of this and a Union drive into central Tennessee toward Nashville, the Confederates lost Kentucky to the Union and much of central and northeastern Tennessee.

Grant was born in Ohio in 1822, and he was raised in Illinois. He was the son of a tanner who believed his son would not amount to much. Grant's father couldn't be blamed, though, as his son showed virtually no interest or talent in anything except horses and riding, at which he absolutely excelled. To give his son direction, his father managed to secure Ulysses an appointment at West Point, where he graduated in the middle of his class in 1843.

In 1846, the United States went to war with Mexico. During the Mexican campaign, Grant, who did not agree with the US cause against Mexico, was assigned as regimental quartermaster of the 4ᵗʰ US Infantry, and he excelled at supply and logistics. He also saw combat at Palo Alto, Resaca, and Monterey, where he distinguished himself in a now-famous ride under fire to deliver a request for ammunition from surrounded troops. During the Mexican-American War, he became acquainted with a number of men he would both serve with and fight against in the Civil War, most famously the future Confederate commander Robert E. Lee.

When the war ended, Grant, who by this time was married with a growing family, held a variety of posts in the East and Midwest, but when he was sent west to California and the Oregon Territory to hold distant and boring posts, he fell into alcoholism. During the Civil War, rumors of Grant being drunk rose from time to time, but it's believed that the only case in which he truly drank to excess was during the long, slow siege of Vicksburg on the Mississippi River in the spring and summer of 1863, a year after Shiloh. At no time was Grant ever accused of being drunk during a battle or at a crucial moment.

Grant quit the army in 1854 and attempted to make it in a variety of businesses and farming; however, all of these attempts failed. The outbreak of the Civil War saw him working as a clerk in his father's saddlery in Illinois. He volunteered for the war effort, and due to his West Point and Mexican-American War experiences, he was shortly made colonel and, a month later, in August 1861, brigadier general. In the fall of 1861, Grant forced Confederate forces to retreat from Paducah, Kentucky. In November, he engaged the Rebels in Missouri and Kentucky, suffering a defeat and winning small victories while also making a name for himself in Washington, especially with President Lincoln, who was suffering from a plethora of generals who had no fight in them. Lincoln liked Grant's pugnacity.

In February 1862, Grant won the Union's first major victories at Forts Henry and Donelson while commanding the Army of the Tennessee. At Fort Donelson, the Confederates within the fort asked for surrender terms. Grant's reply? "Nothing less than unconditional surrender will be accepted." From that moment on, Ulysses S. Grant, or rather "U. S. Grant," was known as "Unconditional Surrender" Grant. Through February and March, Grant gathered men and supplies and, along with Union Western commanding general Henry Halleck, devised a plan to seize the key rail lines in Corinth, Mississippi, just south of the Tennessee border, about 120 miles east of Memphis.

Illustration 9: Grant with an uncharacteristically long beard, which he trimmed just before Shiloh.

Under Grant's command in his campaign to cut the key rail lines at Corinth were a number of other general officers: Lewis "Lew" Wallace (who would write the epic novel *Ben Hur* after the war), Don Carlos Buell (whose Army of the Ohio had just driven the Confederates out of southern Kentucky and the key cities of Clarksville and Nashville), Benjamin Prentiss (who had been a lawyer in Illinois before the war and was a Mexican-American War veteran), another Wallace (this one "W. H. L" for William Hervey Lamme, whose wife made her way to the battlefield to be with her husband), Charles Smith (whose division was probably the best-trained in Grant's army, many of whom had not seen combat), and Stephen Hurlbut (a native North Carolinian who had moved to Illinois before the war).

However, one general stands out from the others: William Tecumseh Sherman. Sherman had just rejoined the army after what was called "a severe bout of melancholia," which we know today as serious mental and emotional depression. Some in the army even called him insane, but Sherman had served with Grant before. He was actually his senior officer by date when they were both brigadiers. Grant and Sherman would be the Union's equivalent to Robert E. Lee and Thomas J. "Stonewall" Jackson, as both pairs of men seemed to know each other's thoughts seemingly before they were spoken and trusted one another implicitly.

In the case of Sherman and Grant, some have surmised the close bond between them stemmed from Sherman's defense of Grant when rumors of his drinking stalled his career just before and early in the war. Grant was one of the few men willing to take Sherman into his command after his serious bout with depression, which lasted about six weeks. Another of Sherman's supporters was the overall Union commander in the West, Henry Halleck, whom Sherman, a West Point graduate, had met during the Mexican-American War.

Sherman was tall, high-strung, and sometimes indecisive before battle, but during the battle, he, like Grant, seemed to develop a sort of preternatural calm, especially when others around him were panicking. When Sherman came to the battlefield at Shiloh, he was in command of some of the greenest troops in the Union Army, some of whom were more than a little leery about having a "crazy man" commanding them.

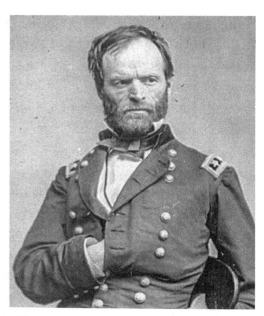

Illustration 10: Sherman in the popular Napoleonic pose of the time, sometime after Shiloh.

Southern Men

The men of the Confederate Army of the Mississippi were commanded by General Albert Sidney Johnston, another West Pointer who had graduated two years behind Confederate President Jefferson Davis, with whom he was good friends. Johnston was a Kentuckian, but he had moved to Texas and took part in the Texas War of Independence. Although he joined as a private, he quickly moved up the ranks to become a senior brigadier general by the end of the war.

An event during this time may actually have cost Johnston his life almost thirty years later at Shiloh. He fought a duel with a fellow general and was shot through the hip, causing nerve damage that caused most of his right leg to go numb. At Shiloh, he was shot behind the right knee, but he paid it little mind until he nearly fell off his horse from the loss of blood—the bullet had severed a branch of his femoral artery, and he bled to death.

Before he met his fate at Shiloh, Johnston was known as the "Man of Three Republics"—he had fought for Texas, serving as its secretary of state during its short independence, the Federal army, and, finally, the Confederacy. Johnston was considered by many in the South to be its greatest general (that is before the rise of Robert E. Lee), but before Shiloh, he had been pushed ever southward by Ulysses S. Grant. At Shiloh, Johnston and his fellow general, P. G. T Beauregard, formulated a plan to push Grant's army against the Tennessee River and destroy it for good.

Illustration 11: Painting of Johnston done at the start of the Civil War.

Beauregard, who had seen to the surrender of Fort Sumter and who had commanded Southern troops at Bull Run, thought himself the equal of Johnston, at least in rank, and superior to him in ability. During the Battle of Shiloh, Beauregard took over after Johnston's death, but a series of key mistakes by both generals may have cost the South the battle. Beauregard led troops throughout the war, in both the East and the West, and survived the conflict. He became a very rich man in New Orleans after the war, helping organize a scheme for the Louisiana lottery, successfully patenting a series of inventions for trolley cars, and becoming a novelist.

At Shiloh, Johnston and Beauregard commanded a force that included units under the command of Leonidas K. Polk (who had been an influential Episcopal bishop in Louisiana before the war), William J. Hardee (known as "Old Reliable"; he was born in 1815 and fought in the Second Seminole War in Florida and the Mexican-American War), John C. Breckinridge (a Kentucky politician and non-combat Mexican-American War veteran who was the youngest vice president in United States history, serving under James Buchanan, and who went on to become the last Confederate secretary of war), and finally Braxton Bragg (who also fought in the Second Seminole War and in Mexico with heroism, saving the unit under the command of one Jefferson Davis, with whom he became fast friends; in fact, Bragg's friendship with Davis may have saved his career during the Civil War, for he could be both competent and grossly incompetent and was known for arguing with just about everyone over everything. At one point later in the war, Confederate cavalry commander Nathan Bedford Forrest, who played a small role at Shiloh, threatened his life).

Chapter 4 – Prelude to the Battle

It was obvious to virtually all of the men in the Confederate Army of the Mississippi that the Union's next move would be to seize the railroad hubs and storage facilities at Corinth, Mississippi.

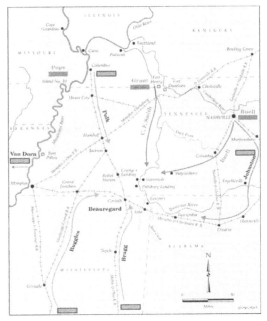

Illustration 12: The situation in western Tennessee/northern Mississippi just before the battle. Courtesy National Park Service.

Corinth, Mississippi, is just south of the Tennessee/Mississippi border where the north-south Mobile and Ohio Railroad and Memphis and Charleston Railroad meet. Of the two, the Memphis and Charleston was the more important, for it was the only railway that led from the Gulf of Mexico to Richmond, the capital of the Confederacy. Cut that line, and the supplies and men going east to west (and vice versa) would have to go by wagon, which would both increase supply times and likely decrease their amount. The Union plan was to sever the western part of the Confederacy from the eastern part and to control the Mississippi, which would allow them to regulate the north-south passage of supplies and cut off the western Confederate states of Texas, Louisiana, and Arkansas from the rest.

Confederate spies and scouts had sent reports stating that the Union Army of the Ohio under Don Carlos Buell had been ordered to march west to rendezvous with the Army of the Tennessee under Grant. If that happened, the Union would outnumber the Confederates in the area by about two to one or more. As it was, Johnston was able to concentrate about fifty-five thousand men for the coming battle.

The Rebels took the idea of losing Corinth so seriously that they summoned virtually all of their troops stationed in Louisiana north to Corinth, leaving (unbeknownst to the Federals) New Orleans wide open. Among these troops was Brigadier General Daniel Ruggles's artillery. He was born in 1810, graduated from West Point, and fought in the Second Seminole War and in Mexico, where he became acquainted with many of the men on the battlefield of Shiloh, including U. S. Grant. He had also fought with Albert Sidney Johnston during the Mormon Uprising in Utah. Ruggles would play a key role on the first day of Shiloh.

Similarly, General Leonidas Polk, who oversaw two divisions, was summoned from the fortified but poorly located Columbus, Kentucky, which he had seized in an attempt to prevent Union control of the Mississippi and which was now almost completely behind enemy lines.

Also joining the forces converging on Pittsburg Landing were Tennessean Benjamin Cheatham's some three thousand men. Benjamin Cheatham was a hard-fighting officer from Nashville who had also fought in the Mexican-American War and who, after the Civil War in his old age, would supervise much of the landscaping at Arlington National Cemetery, Robert E. Lee's former home.

In the middle of March, Grant began to move his forces southward. His headquarters were to be at Savannah, Tennessee, about nine miles north of the battlefield. When he arrived in Savannah, he set up his headquarters in William H. Cherry's mansion. Cherry was a pro-Union Tennessean, of which there were many, though most were located in the eastern part of the state.

When Grant arrived in Savannah, he found Union Brigadier General Charles Ferguson Smith's troops. Smith's forces were located on both sides of the Tennessee River, so Grant ordered them to be brought over by some of the 170 steamboats that he had taken upriver. The next day, Grant began deploying his troops southward. Five divisions would land at Pittsburg Landing (named after a whiskey maker named Pitt, who sold his product to the rivermen on the Tennessee before the war) about nine miles upriver from Savannah (the Tennessee River flows from south to north, so "upriver" is actually moving southward, against the current). One of Grant's divisions, under Lew Wallace, would be stationed to the west of Savannah on the western side of the river at Crump's Landing. In total, Grant had just under forty-three thousand men under his command.

Grant's superior, Henry Halleck, was concerned that Grant might do something rash before Buell's troops made their way to him, so he ordered Grant "to avoid a general engagement." Grant replied that he would not engage the enemy but that it would likely be impossible to avoid contact with the Rebels as he marched toward Corinth. Perhaps this made Halleck a bit nervous, for he reiterated sometime later that Grant and his generals were not to move until Buell arrived. "By all means keep your forces together until you connect with General Buell. Do not let the enemy draw you into an engagement now." Buell's forces numbered about thirty thousand men. When they did arrive, Grant would have the numerical advantage.

This fact was known to Johnston and Beauregard, who decided that rather than wait for Grant to besiege them in Corinth with twice as many men and more guns, food, and other supplies, they would attempt to surprise him at Pittsburg Landing, cut him off from the river and Buell, and destroy him. Once that was done, they could turn on the smaller forces of Buell and deal with him as well.

Speed was the key. But the Confederates were faced with a number of problems before they could get to Pittsburg Landing and fight Grant.

The Confederate forces near Corinth were made up of green troops, many of whom had had very little training at all. Although this problem plagued the Union as well, the Confederates suffered from it more. Even the basic commands of the complicated group maneuvers were new to them, and they were expected to march over twenty miles and enter a fight against a general who was on a winning streak.

Late on April 2nd, 1862, Johnston and Beauregard got word that Buell's army was approaching Savannah. Beauregard told Johnston, "Now is the time to go," for if Buell united with Grant, their plans were over. Johnston agreed, and the two set the ball in motion. They had hoped to be joined by General Earl van Dorn's army, which was somewhere on the other side of the Mississippi in Arkansas, but the generals in Corinth could not wait any longer. Either Van Dorn hadn't been found by the messengers they sent out, wasn't coming, or couldn't come or make it on time.

Johnston's plan was a good one. His orders for the men under his command were as follows: "In the approaching battle, every effort should be made to turn the left flank of the enemy, so as to cut off his line of retreat to the Tennessee River and throw him back on Owl Creek [a nearby wide and swollen body of water that would be impossible to cross in battle] where he will be obliged to surrender." Johnston hoped to get his army squared away (fed, supplied with ammunition, etc.), move out at dawn on the 3rd, march the twenty-plus miles, and attack Grant at Pittsburg Landing on April 4th.

His units were to march to a junction called Mickey's about eight miles south of Pittsburg Landing, overnight there, and attack the next morning, on April 4th. Even though Johnston was nominally in command, he and Beauregard seemed to have split duties, with Johnston making sure the plan was set and that the wheels were turning and with Beauregard planning the line of march and its coordination.

Johnston and Beauregard had about 28,000 men with them at Corinth, and these would be joined by about 12,000 more, which would all converge at Mickey's. General Bragg commanded 16,000 men, and General Hardee had just over 6,700. Breckinridge brought his corps that numbered 7,200 men, and Benjamin Cheatham brought 5,000 from the northwest.

The Confederate forces numbered just over forty thousand men (including some four thousand cavalry), which was about equal to Grant's force. Conventional military wisdom called for the attacking force to have at least a two-to-one advantage over the defenders, but in most situations during the Civil War, this was a luxury the men of the South simply did not have. The population of the Union states was twenty million. The population of the Confederacy was eight million, and while the Rebels were quite successful in raising an army much larger than should have been possible (after all, the bulk of their labor force consisted of millions of enslaved people), Confederate officers often relied on maneuvers, surprise, and unorthodox tactics to offset the Union's numerical superiority. It would have to be this way at Shiloh too.

With thousands of green troops at a time when orders were passed by written notes that were handed off personally or came by word of mouth, the CSA camp was slow and uncoordinated as it moved out on April 3rd. If you've watched movies about the Civil War or even the Napoleonic Wars, not much is said about the skill and timing needed to coordinate a march of twenty miles, much less an attack, especially at a time with very archaic communications systems. Of course, it would not be a very exciting movie. In order to reach the battlefield in a way in which troops can stay with their units, the order of battle deemed most effective by their generals had veteran troops arriving first, with their support, ammunition, and artillery right behind them, followed by less experienced troops, etc. Another question for the commanders would be which general did they want as the "point of the spear" of their attack? Perhaps there were veteran units commanded by a general who excelled at defense but who was hesitant on the attack, while another more inexperienced unit was led by more aggressive officers, etc.

Making things worse, it was spring in Tennessee, and while it had not gotten overly warm yet, the rain was a problem. It was not raining on April 2nd, but the roads were still sloppy from prior rainfall, which slowed things down before the men could even approach Mickey's. All of this combined to get the Confederates off to a very slow start, the first of many misfortunes that may have cost the Rebels the battle. By the close of the day on April 3rd, the lead Confederate forces set up camp some miles short of Mickey's. Making things worse, the road leading back to Corinth was clogged all the way back to the town with the rest of the army. Men had to fall out by the side of the road and rest as best they could.

The next day, Friday, April 4th, the day originally designated for the attack, brought rain—and lots of it. The ground was already wet, but now, it had become a quagmire. The roads in the rural area were all dirt roads and wagon tracks, and soon, they dissolved into nothing but mud. The route to Pittsburg Landing became a veritable swamp, which made walking difficult, not to mention horse-drawn wagons and cannons. The effort to move just a few miles did nothing but make the men tired.

Worse still, many of the men had already gone through the three days' rations they had been given the day before. Hunger from the exertion, the cold rain, boredom, and the weight of the rations all combined to cause many of the men to consume what they had on them, and they would go into battle on an empty stomach, which would have consequences during the fight.

It kept raining, delaying things another day, and on the night of April 5th, Johnston walked into a meeting of his commanders (Beauregard, Polk, Bragg, and soon to be joined by Breckinridge) and discussed the situation. Although they had been initially fired up for the attack, both Beauregard and Bragg were now against it. They suggested to Johnston that since Union cavalry and other scouts had engaged some of the Confederate pickets (small forces sent out to guard/watch the approaches to the main camp), Grant must know they were there and probably already prepared fortifications. Bragg and Beauregard argued that if that was the case, then an attack would be futile, and the Confederates needed to come up with another plan.

Johnston and Polk disagreed. Scouts, spies, and civilians in the area had reported that Grant's men were not entrenched anywhere and that the Union Army was still at Pittsburg Landing. What's more, Buell had not joined them yet. After some deliberation, Johnston gave the order. "We shall attack at daylight tomorrow!" Since the battle, many believe that Johnston was overly concerned with his reputation. His forces had been driven south by Grant, he had sustained two large and humiliating defeats, and the Northerners were driving into the heart of the Confederacy. After he gave the order, Johnston strode outside and met his brother-in-law, Brigadier General William

Preston, and said, "I would fight them if they were a million." Perhaps Johnston was too carried away.

In actuality, the civilians, scouts, and spies reporting to Johnston were correct. Grant and his generals, particularly Sherman, had no idea that the Confederates were only a few miles away. Practically all of the Union commanders believed that the reports of a large Confederate concentration at and around Corinth meant that there would be a hard fight ahead when the Union men assaulted that important rail junction. They dismissed a number of reports coming in that told them the Confederates were much closer than that.

In Grant's mind, he would assault Corinth in overwhelming force, cut the Confederacy in half, and perhaps end the war. Also on his mind were Halleck's orders to not provoke a fight with the Rebels until Buell's army had united with Grant's. Therefore, the scouts and pickets sent out by Grant and his commanders did not venture very far from the main camp near the Tennessee River; they went just far enough to make sure the Rebels weren't too close but not far enough to perhaps accidentally run into a larger Confederate force and provoke a battle. Grant was so sure that no Confederates were "north of Corinth" (as his friend Sherman put it) that he hadn't even had his men dig in, thinking this might cause them to think defensively and worry that their commander had turned into a copy of one of those Union commanders in the East. Anyway, he planned to move out for Corinth soon.

Even so, some of the Union pickets reported hearing large groups of men in the distance and saw large groups of cavalry go by between wooded thickets not far to the south. In actuality, despite orders to the contrary from Johnston and most Confederate officers to keep quiet, many of the green troops, eager for their chance to "whup those Yankees," shouted, joked, and played the drums; some even blew trumpets or bugles. Little skirmishes between small groups of men in the area of Pittsburg Landing had been going on since the 3rd, and on the afternoon of the 4th, Union troops reported being fired on by a

Confederate cannon. These reports were dismissed as local skirmishes with Confederate scouts sent to probe and see if Grant was moving toward Corinth. Even Sherman, known later in the war for his aggressiveness, dismissed the reports as the product of inexperienced officers' overactive imaginations, replying to one, "Oh, tut, tut! You militia officers get scared too easily."

On the morning of April 6th, 1862, with dawn appearing faintly on the horizon, the Confederates began to move into place for their attack on Grant's positions near Pittsburg Landing. On the Union's right and the Confederate's left stood a little log Methodist church, which had been built nine years before. It was called Shiloh, Hebrew for "place of peace."

Illustration 13: Inside of the Shiloh church today. Courtesy Matthew Gaskill.

Chapter 5 – The Battle

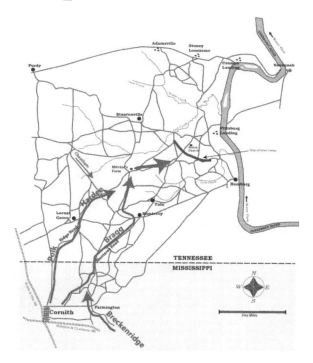

Illustration 14: The Confederate approach to Shiloh. "Michie's Farm" is and was pronounced and spelled "Mickey's" by the soldiers on both sides. The main Union line is labeled in blue, with the Shiloh church directly behind it.

Sherman's troops were on the right flank of the Union line west of the Shiloh church. On that line was one of the nervous officers that Sherman was referring to in his quote above. This officer was Colonel Jesse Appler, who commanded the 53rd Ohio Regiment. Appler was too old to be on a battlefield, and he was the nervous type, but on Saturday afternoon, he had sent pickets farther afield than most of the other Union officers because of that nervousness. His troops were green and untrained, but they knew Confederates when they saw them, so they came back to Appler, saying that they had been fired on by a "line of men in butternut clothes," which they had. Those Confederate troops were the pickets of General Hardee's division. More reports were dismissed by other Union commanders as the fears of untried men. Still, Sherman did send Grant, who was rehabbing at Cherry Mansion in Savannah, having sprained an ankle the day before, a message, saying that he believed that two regiments, some cavalry, and a few cannons were about two miles away. He proposed capturing some Rebels and sending them back to Grant for questioning. Later on Saturday, Sherman wrote another dispatch to Grant, worded in the language typical of the time: "I have no doubt that nothing will occur today more than some picket firing...The enemy is saucy, but got the worst of it yesterday...I do not apprehend anything like an attack on our position." Interestingly enough, Sherman mentioned to a nearby reporter that he did think danger was near. The reporter asked Sherman why he did not report it, to which the tall, red-headed general replied, "Oh, they'd just say I was crazy again."

At 4:55 a.m. on Sunday, in the middle of the Union line, another officer was feeling the hairs on the back of his neck stand up. Colonel Everett Peabody, an engineer and railroad executive before the war and who was now in command of the 25th Missouri Volunteer Regiment, was alarmed by a report given by his cavalry commander, Major James E. Powell, which stated that an astounding number of Confederate campfires were seen not far from their position. Peabody ordered Powell to take about three hundred cavalry troopers and reconnoiter the area.

At the edge of a field about a half-mile from their lines, Prentiss's troopers ran headlong into the men of the Confederate 3rd Mississippi Infantry Battalion, commanded by Major Aaron Hardcastle. This was part of the brigade commanded by Brigadier Sterling M. Wood, which included men from Tennessee, Alabama, and Arkansas. The Rebels fired on Prentiss's dismounted men and fell back. The Federals moved forward, firing a volley, until they saw what no one had suspected—about nine thousand Rebels in gray and butternut, kneeling on a rise just ahead. Just then, one of the Mississippi men fired and killed Lieutenant Frederick Klinger. He would be the first casualty of what would become the bloodiest day of the war to that point.

Illustration 15: Where Powell met the Rebels. The ground was less manicured in 1862. Courtesy Matthew Gaskill.

The Confederates advanced on a narrow front as they approached the Union front lines. Hardee's corps marched in two ranks, one unit behind another, which was followed by the horses, wagons, and men of the artillery straining to pull heavy guns on the muddy dirt roads. Then came Bragg's large corps made up of five brigades, which were also in ranks of two. These were followed by the men of Polk's corps, who formed deeper ranks about a mile behind, and these were followed by Breckinridge's men, whose troops would serve as a reserve to go where and when they might be needed most. From the point where the Mississippi men met Powell back, the Confederate Army stretched almost two miles to the rear.

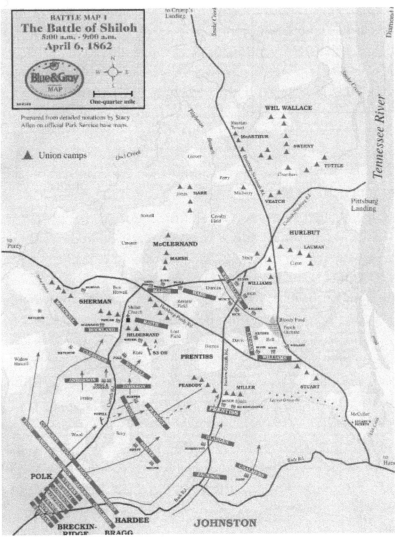

Illustration 16: First hours of Shiloh showing CSA approach and dispersal. Courtesy National Park Service.

To the rear of Powell's fight with the Confederate vanguard was Colonel Peabody, who ordered reinforcements to be sent forward. But as they moved toward Powell, they were greeted by the sight of his retreating troopers, who were, in turn, followed by the mass of the Confederate Army of the Mississippi. At that, the officers in Peabody's camp ordered the alarm to be sounded, and drum rolls pealed through the Union camp. As they fell into some sort of order and prepared their weapons, their commanding general, Benjamin Prentiss, rode up to Peabody, yelling to be heard over the commotion. "Colonel Peabody, I will hold you personally responsible for bringing on this engagement!" To which Peabody replied that he was always responsible for his actions. It was lucky for the Union that Peabody had sent Powell forward, for if he had not, the first thing greeting the Union men in his camp would have been thousands of fired-up Rebels.

On the Confederate side, General Beauregard, who was getting the lay of the land and was familiar with the road conditions, still wanted to call off the attack, especially after knowing the Yankees had been alerted. At this point, it was too late. By the time orders went out and the men pulled back and sorted out, it's likely the Union would have been upon them. Instead of being on the attack against mostly unsuspecting troops or in Corinth in fortified positions, the Rebels would be on open and unfamiliar ground, with green troops attempting to fall back under fire. No, Johnston would have none of it, and he ordered Beauregard and the army to press on. "Tonight we will water our horses in the Tennessee!" he exclaimed.

Johnston told Beauregard to remain in the rear and organize the advance and direct supplies and reinforcements as they would be needed. He would advance with the troops and help coordinate the attack, which, as he had telegraphed Jefferson Davis earlier, would consist of "Polk in the left, Bragg the center, Hardee the right and Breckinridge in reserve." Johnston's plan was for Hardee to advance up the line of the river to cut off the Union from the escape route across it while the rest of his forces pressed the Union eastward in a large vise. For his part, it seems that Beauregard was on board with part of that idea, but he wanted to sweep the Union men eastward against the river and destroy them. As you can see, coordination of the Confederate command was lacking at Shiloh.

It was made worse when Albert Sidney Johnston rode forward with the attack. It was textbook, then and now, that an army commander should not put himself in harm's way, especially at the start of a battle. He should have remained in the rear, assigned aides to ride forward, and coordinate the Rebel attack from a safe position. No one is exactly sure why Johnston took the action he did on April 6th, and what's more, he followed the troops on the far Confederate right (the Union left) at the point farthest from the rest (and the majority) of his army. Perhaps he thought he should be at what he considered the lynchpin of his plan, cutting off the Union from the river. Maybe he thought that his presence would spur his men on; after all, he was a popular commander. Or perhaps he was eager to be in the field when he got his revenge against Grant for the defeats at Forts Henry and Donelson. Whatever the reason, he left Beauregard, who was hesitant about the attack and had different plans, in command and moved forward, at one point in the battle sending his own personal physician to the rear to aid wounded men and giving his own tourniquet to a wounded man on the field.

On the Union right, where Brigadier General William Tecumseh Sherman's 5th Division was positioned and where the nervous Colonel Appler of the 53rd Ohio had been raising the alarm for days, men started streaming northward from where Appler and his men had been hearing ever increasing and approaching fire. One man with his arm badly mangled ran past Appler and his aide, Lieutenant Ephraim Dawes, screaming, "Get into line! The Rebels are coming!" Appler ordered the men around him forward to form a skirmish line and sent another message to Sherman. Rearward, Sherman had had it with Appler's nervousness, and when the messenger returned to the older man, that was made clear. Sherman replied, "You must be badly scared over there." The timing of Sherman's message could not have been more ironically perfect, for as Appler and Dawes heard Sherman's reply, they saw hundreds of men advancing on their right, polished gun barrels glinting in the glare of the rising sun.

At that, Appler exclaimed, "This is no place for us!" and sounded the retreat, which, despite the colonel's semi-panic, was exactly the right call to make. After retreating back some distance from their camp, Appler's men took up a good position on the top of a bush-covered rise and waited for the Rebels to come closer.

Sherman knew that Confederates were in the area, but he was convinced that what Appler saw was simply a reconnaissance in force. Nonetheless, he rode forward to see for himself. When he arrived at Appler's position, he looked through his binoculars and realized that Appler was right, but before he had time to react, a lieutenant named Eustace Ball yelled out to him, "General, look to your right!" Just then, some Rebel sharpshooters rose up about fifty yards from his position and opened fire. Sherman exclaimed, "My God! We are attacked!" and threw up a hand to protect his face as the Rebels fired. Sherman's orderly, Private Thomas Holliday of the 2nd Illinois Cavalry, took a fatal bullet and fell from his horse. Sherman was wounded in the hand, and as he rapidly backed away, he told his nervous colonel, "Appler, hold your position, I will support you," then galloped off. Sherman's behavior was unusual, but he would lead his men bravely and smartly for the rest of the battle.

Appler did hold his position for quite a while. The Confederates mounted a number of attacks across the rough ravine in front of his position. These men were led by an outstanding Southern general named Patrick Cleburne, who had immigrated from Ireland and had fought with the British Army before doing so. Cleburne would go on to fight in some of the major battles to follow in the West, but that morning, he and his troops found themselves struggling against muddy, swampy terrain covered in tree stumps and roots on that ravine in front of the 53rd Ohio. This caused his formation to split into two sections, with Cleburne in command of the one thousand men (the 23rd Tennessee and 6th Mississippi) in front of Appler, with the rest of his brigade getting scattered through the thick woods, something that was beginning to happen throughout the Confederate line.

Appler's men opened up on the Southerners as they entered the former Union camp. Behind his riflemen, the 1st Illinois Light Artillery opened fire on the Rebels. Cleburne later reported, "Musketry and artillery at short range swept the open spaces between the tents, with an iron storm that threatened certain destruction for every living thing that dared to cross." The 23rd Tennessee broke under the fire. Cleburne rallied about half of the men from the Tennessee brigade and half from the Mississippi brigade and moved forward, screaming the notorious "Rebel yell." Another blast reduced his ranks even further, but the Rebels kept coming, even though they were being destroyed in the process. After the second push by the Rebels, Appler called a retreat, and many of his men ran away in panic, though two companies of men remained in position under the command of Lieutenant Dawes.

All across the Confederate left (Union right), the Rebels came on and on, but the Union men under Sherman on the far right and Prentiss to his left fought desperately to hold their ground. The Rebels had hoped that Hardee's men would break through the Union lines, but that was not happening. Bragg's corps, with nearly sixteen thousand men, moved to the left to press the attack.

If you ever visit the Shiloh National Battlefield, perhaps the first thing that will strike you is its size—it's very small, only 5.8 square miles. Within this space, eighty thousand men were crammed together in fields, woods, and ravines, fighting to the death. No wonder the death toll was so high. When walking the grounds, it is hard to imagine eighty thousand men fitting into the area, much less fighting, but they did.

As the battle grew in intensity between 6 and 7 a.m., Ulysses S. Grant was taking breakfast at the Cherry Mansion in Savannah just a few miles away. He heard the rumble of guns and walked out onto the porch of the house to listen. He turned to his men, limping past them on his sprained ankle, saying, "Gentlemen, the ball is in motion. Let's be off." Before he went aboard his personal steamboat, the *Tigress*, he sent two notes for reinforcements: one to Buell, urging him to hurry, and the other to Brigadier General William Nelson, whose 4th Division of the Army of the Ohio was already filing onto the eastern bank of the Tennessee. Grant ordered Nelson to move south along the east bank opposite Pittsburg Landing, where some of the many steamboats with his forces would meet Nelson and bring them across the river to join the fight. This may have been an error on Grant's part because he could have ordered Nelson's troops to be brought on board the ferries at Savannah so they could be steamed upriver (remember, the Tennessee flows south to north) to Pittsburg Landing rather than have them march south for nine miles first, but that is what happened.

Illustration 17: Pittsburg Landing today looking north toward Savannah. Courtesy Matthew Gaskill.

Illustration 18: Grant's personal riverboat, the Tigress *(center), at Pittsburg Landing shortly after the battle.*

Before Grant got to Pittsburg Landing, he stopped just a short ride away at Crump's Landing, where he had stationed Lew Wallace and his 3rd Division and told them to prepare to move. Wallace told Grant that he had heard cannon fire and that he had made his men ready, but Grant did not give him orders to move at this time. He likely should have, for later in the day, a series of confusing events involving Wallace, his reception of spoken over written orders, and his unfamiliarity with the terrain would lead to his delay in getting to the battlefield.

Farther south, General Prentiss and Colonel Peabody were taking the brunt of the Confederate attack. General Johnston had arrived and ordered the Rebels to mount a massive bayonet charge across about three hundred yards of relatively open field. Though they sustained high casualties and the Union men fought hard, the Rebels' charge, which was accompanied by thousands of men giving the notorious "Rebel yell," broke the men in Prentiss's position, causing many of them to panic. These men, soon to be joined by others in Federal units nearby, fled all the way back to Pittsburg Landing.

Nothing could stop them, and nothing, from threats to calm reassurance, could get most of them to return to the front lines. Worse still, the men from Prentiss's division, many of them bloody with their own blood or the blood of others, ran through units coming up from the rear, sowing panic among a good many of them, especially among the green troops. "We're cut to pieces! The Rebels are coming! We're whipped!" were only some of the cries that went up. (As a side note, in the bibliography, you can find a link to an old newsreel of very old Confederate veterans giving the crowd a much appreciated "Rebel yell.")

While the Southerners victoriously pushed Prentiss's back in the center and sent hundreds panicking to the rear, they may have also cost the Confederacy the battle. On the march to Shiloh, many of the untrained and ill-disciplined men had gone through their rations and had not had anything to eat for over twenty-four hours. The shock and quickness of their attack had been such a surprise that the men in Prentiss's camp (almost two brigades of them) had just woken up, which means hundreds of cook fires were still burning with pots full of soup, bacon, biscuits, and hot coffee. At that point, hordes of hungry Rebels stopped in their tracks and began to loot the Union camp. Not only did they help themselves to the Yankees' food, but they also began looting personal belongings that had been left behind and even engaged in debates over whether Southern or Northern women were more attractive.

Even General Johnston, the highest-ranking Confederate soldier in the West and the second-highest in the whole army (Adjutant and Inspector General Samuel Cooper was the highest), could not get the Rebels moving again. When he saw one of his officers emerge from a Union tent with an armful of loot, he scolded him, saying, "None of that, sir! We are not here for plunder!" The officer gave Johnston a chastened look, and the general then picked up a Union tin cup and said, "Let this be my share of the spoils for the day." Johnston held the cup and used it as a pointer for the rest of his life, which was soon to be coming to an end.

Illustration 19: The site of Prentiss's main camp today with historical marker telling the story of the looting that went on there. Courtesy Matthew Gaskill.

Though many of Prentiss's men had panicked, he and his officers were able to gather together about one thousand men along an old wagon track dividing a dense thicket to the rear and slightly east of his original position. At about that time, Union general Stephen Hurlbut sent two of his brigades to aid Prentiss along what became (and is now) known as the "Sunken Road." His third brigade was sent to reinforce Sherman's forces on the right.

If you refer to the map a few pages back, you'll see that Prentiss's original position was in the center of the Union line. When his position was lost, Sherman was forced to order his brigade commanders to pull back, lest the Rebels drive past the Union left and catch the Yankees in a vise. This was at about 9 a.m., and the battle had been going on for a good four hours already. Sherman gave an aide this message: "Tell Grant if he has any men to spare I can use them. If not, I will do the best I can. We are holding them pretty well just now. Pretty well; but it's hot as hell."

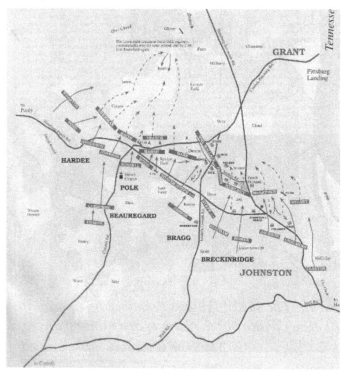

Illustration 20: The battle between 11 a.m. and 2 p.m. Courtesy Blue & Gray Magazine.

At this time, Grant was sending messages to Lew Wallace to "hurry up your command as fast as possible," but a series of misunderstandings delayed Wallace's movement, and when he did move, he took the wrong road. A march that should have taken him two hours at most ended up taking nearly seven. However, though Wallace's men did not take part in the battle on Sunday, they and Nelson's troops, who were also being hurried by Grant but did not arrive until sunset, would be fresh for the fight on Monday. They had twenty thousand fresh men, plus what Grant already had against the

Confederates, who were fully committed with no reinforcements available.

Throughout the morning, on the Rebel left and center, the back-and-forth fighting and repeated charges, combined with the thick undergrowth and woods, smoke from the guns, and the confusion that comes in every battle, caused the Confederate forces to become intermingled. Commanders lost their men and vice versa. Men from Mississippi were fighting in units made up of Tennesseans, with different combinations like this happening all along the line. The Rebel generals conferred in person or through messengers and decided, after some time, that commanders would no longer be responsible for their units but for those men who fell within certain areas. Even this was ineffective to a large degree, and the chain of command broke down. This happened to a lesser degree in the Union ranks, but by noon, the fighting at Shiloh had become a "soldier's fight," with lieutenants, sergeants, corporals, and veteran privates leading the men nearby.

Despite Johnston's plan, most of the fighting took place in the center and left of their line. The original plan called for the main Rebel thrust to move near the river to cut off the Union line of retreat and force their surrender or annihilate them. However, as the battle evolved and as the confusion grew, more and more units from both sides followed the most basic of orders: go where the firing was. In the morning and early afternoon, most of the fighting was done at the center and left. What's more, the units that were assigned to push along the river were unfamiliar with the area, and between the thick growth and the deep ravines, which were oftentimes filled partly with water, the Rebels' field of view was limited. They could not see the river, but they believed they were pushing toward it, but this was because their maps were aligned incorrectly. Had they been able to continue their push forward later in the day, they would have ended up a few hundred yards inland, far from their objective.

In the center of the line, the 1,000 men under General Prentiss, which had combined with the roughly 1,500 reinforcements under the command of General W. H. L Wallace, took up positions in the woods in front of the Sunken Road. After a short lull, in which both sides attempted to reorganize their men and come up with a strategy going forward, the fighting in the center picked up again around 12:30, and it soon became absolutely ferocious.

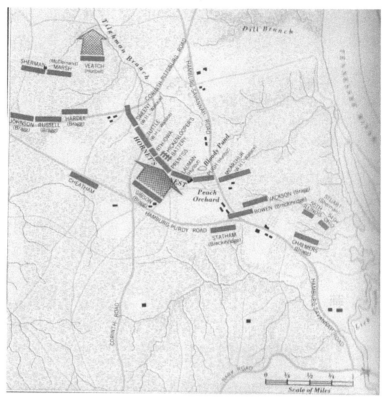

Illustration 21: The situation around 1 p.m. The "Hornet's Nest" is in the center. Courtesy Time-Life Books.

At 12:30, Confederate colonel Randall Gibson moved his 13th Louisiana Infantry brigade (of Bragg's corps), along with what men he gathered, and launched the first of what would be about a dozen Confederate attacks on Prentiss's position. The first attack, which was met with thousands of rifles supported by cannons, was bloodily repulsed, as were the next and the next and the next. Soon, the Rebels in the area were calling this position the "Hornet's Nest" for the sound of thousands of rounds buzzing through the air.

One of the men in the Hornet's Nest was Colonel Peabody, who had ordered Major Powell forward earlier in the morning. Peabody sustained three wounds when a Minié ball hit him in the face, killing him instantly. Major Powell had also fallen by that time.

Illustration 22: General Prentiss.

Illustration 23: Colonel Gibson.

Illustration 24: Colonel Peabody.

Throughout the day, more and more Confederate troops were ordered to or gravitated toward the Hornet's Nest. Gibson's men moved into the Hornet's Nest three times, only to be cut to pieces. More and more Confederates then took their place. Along the Union right, General Stephen Hurlbut moved into position to prevent the Rebels from driving through a gap in the Federal lines, but by late afternoon, he was pushed back. On both sides of the Hornet's Nest, Rebel troops moved in, yet Wallace's and Prentiss's men held on.

This began to change at about 4:30 when Brigadier General Daniel Ruggles moved almost sixty cannons about three hundred yards from the Hornet's Nest. This was the largest concentration of artillery on the North American continent to that point. They opened at this relatively close range, sending explosive balls and canister into the Hornet's Nest.

Illustration 25: Looking into the Hornet's Nest from the south today. Courtesy Matthew Gaskill.

Illustration 26: Ruggle's position today with the Hornet's Nest in the distance. Some fifty-five cannons sit at the Shiloh Battlefield today. Courtesy Matthew Gaskill.

By 5 p.m., elements of fourteen of the sixteen Confederate brigades on the battlefield that day began to surround the Hornet's Nest. By this time, the Union men inside the Hornet's Nest had begun to retreat from the area before the Confederate trap could close on them.

As they moved to the rear, Union General W. H. L Wallace was hit in the back of the head with a Minié ball, which exited from his left eye socket. The men surrounding him, including his brother-in-law, attempted to bring him to the rear, but the fighting was so severe and his wound so horrible that they had to leave him on the field for dead. Amazingly, the next day, he was alive found by advancing Union troops. His wife, Ann, had traveled to Savannah from Illinois before the battle, unbeknownst to her husband, and had arrived at Pittsburg Landing the night before, the beneficiary of a special pass signed by Ulysses S. Grant. Her husband's brigade chaplain brought her the news of Wallace's death as she attempted to aid wounded men on the many steamboats that acted as makeshift hospitals. The next day, she was told that her husband had been found and was still alive, but barely. For the next three days, she sat with him as he flowed in and out of consciousness. On the third day, he squeezed her hand tightly, looked at her with his good eye, and passed away.

As the Confederate ring tightened, Prentiss realized that escape was impossible and that a relief force was not coming. He and his officers ordered the men remaining in the Hornet's Nest to surrender. Over two thousand Union troops gave themselves up. Later that evening, Prentiss was afforded the treatment his rank was due and dined with Beauregard and other Rebel generals. Beauregard, who famously sent a telegraph back to Jefferson Davis that the Confederacy had won a "complete victory," chuckled when Prentiss told him and the others, "You gentlemen have had your way today but it will be very different tomorrow. You'll see! Buell will effect a junction with Grant tonight and turn the tables on you tomorrow." Prentiss was later exchanged for Confederate officers, and he fought on until he retired in 1863, feeling that, despite being lauded as a hero by Grant and the press, the desk-bound higher-ups had it in for him, as they kept posting him to camps away from the action.

At about the same time that evening, Confederate cavalry Colonel Nathan Bedford Forrest dressed some of his troopers in captured Union clothing and told them to scout the Union lines. He reported what they told him to his brigade commander, General Ronald Chalmers, that the Union was "receiving reinforcements by the thousands, and if this army does not move between this and daylight, it will be whipped like hell before 10 o'clock tomorrow." His report went up the line, but he heard nothing. At 2 a.m., he scouted the Union position himself and returned to camp, excitedly reporting what he had seen to General Hardee, who had been asleep. Hardee merely told Forrest to "keep a bright lookout" and rolled over. By all accounts, Forrest was mad enough to murder.

At 2 p.m., though, that was all in the future. On the Confederate left, General Cheatham's troops, along with elements of Bragg's corps, had begun pushing Sherman's and General John A. McClernand's forces back toward Pittsburg Landing. It was at this point that elements of the Confederates' left began to head toward the firing in the Hornet's Nest, but enough of them continued pressing the Union men on the left, back closer to the Tennessee River. As you can see from the last map, Sherman's and McClernand's forces retreated toward Tilghman's Branch, a wide creek that was even fuller due to the heavy rains from the last days. The position was an excellent one for defense; in addition to the swollen creek, the Federals sat upon a steep rise leading up from the water on the other side.

After attempting to reorganize their troops, the Confederates began to assault Sherman's position across Tilghman's. Each time they were torn to pieces. It was there that the Confederate advance would halt later that afternoon.

On the Confederate right, which was supposed to have been the focus of the battle, fighting was taking place within a peach orchard (now known to history simply as the "Peach Orchard") to the left of Prentiss's position in the Hornet's Nest. These ten acres of blooming peach trees would have been the ideal spot for a picnic. The wind was blowing slightly, and peach blossoms were floating down to the ground. By the end of the day, the trees had been torn apart, the blossoms soaked with blood and trampled into the mud.

General Johnston had moved along the center of his line earlier in the day, attempting to organize attacks, instructing officers, and trying to make sure ammunition went where it was needed. By about 2 p.m., he was at the left of his line, pushing his men forward in an attempt to drive them between the Union men and the river, about half a mile to the east.

The men of General Breckinridge had attempted to push the Yankees out of the Peach Orchard quite a few times, but by the time Johnston arrived, the dead, wounded, and pieces of men from both sides littered the ground. Confederate officers were running about, trying to get their men in order for yet another attack when Johnston came riding up. He called out, "Men! They are stubborn! We must use the bayonet!" And as the men formed ranks, he rode in front of them, tapping each bayonet with his tin cup souvenir as he rode by. Then he moved in front of them, yelling, "I will lead you!"

Seemingly, Johnston's presence and his ability to organize and calm the officers lit a fire under the units in front of the Peach Orchard. He spurred his horse onward, and he and his men charged at almost full-speed into the guns of the Union men defending the area. The Rebels, whooping and howling the Rebel yell, were unstoppable this time. They tore through the orchard and began pushing the surviving Yankees backward, as the map below illustrates.

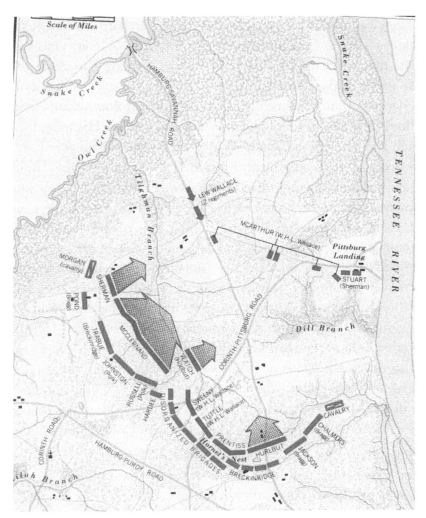

Illustration 27: The situation at Shiloh at about 2 to 3 p.m.

Just north of the Peach Orchard was a small pond. The men from both sides quickly gave it a name—"Bloody Pond." As the battle flowed around them, wounded men from both sides, some missing limbs, others with their entrails dragging behind them, pulled themselves to slake their thirst brought on by the loss of blood. Many died at its banks, and soon, the entire pond was red from the hundreds of men lying around it.

After leading the charge into the Peach Orchard, Johnston came riding back to the Confederate rear, his shirt torn in many places from bullets that had whizzed closely by without striking him. One of his thigh-length riding boots had been struck in the sole so that its heel was flapping under Johnston's stirrup. At first, Johnston appeared to be fired up, then suddenly he reeled in his saddle. His aide, former Tennessee Governor Isham Harris, who had volunteered to be Johnston's aide, jumped onto Johnston's horse behind him, holding the general up with one arm. He asked, "General, are you hurt"? Johnston replied, "Yes, and I fear seriously." Harris took the general into a shallow ravine nearby and helped him off his horse. As was mentioned earlier, Johnston had left his personal doctor with the wounded at another spot on the battlefield and had also given his tourniquet to another soldier to aid a wounded comrade. Harris searched Johnston's body and couldn't find anything until he saw that the general's right boot was leaking blood. Johnston had been wounded behind the right knee. The numbness in his leg had caused him to either not feel it or dismiss it as a light wound, but the bullet had nicked a branch of the key femoral artery. Within minutes, he was dead. Albert Sidney Johnston was the highest-ranking officer of either side to fall on the battlefield in the entire Civil War.

The men of the Union fell back on the Owl Creek Ravine, north of the Peach Orchard. The ravine was over one hundred feet deep with a steep slope. There, they received reinforcements from Grant, including cannons that were loaded with canister and double-canister. In the assaults that followed, the few Confederates that managed to make it out of the ravine were blown off its slopes by short-range cannon and musket fire. Most of the men trying to dislodge the men in blue at Owl Creek were stopped cold in the ravine, many of them caught in a crossfire from hell where the ravine took a turn. Making things worse for the Confederates near the river were two Union gunboats, which began shelling them throughout the rest of the day and into the night.

All through the day, Grant wondered with increasing anger as to where Lew Wallace and his brigade were. He sent a messenger back to Crump's Landing in the late morning. It took him some time to find Wallace in the first place, and when he did, he was given the inexplicable reply that Wallace would only respond to orders in writing. Riding back to Grant, his messenger explained the situation to the general, who fumed and authorized his aide to write out orders to Wallace in his name. Two more messengers were sent back to Wallace to no avail—the general, whose troops fought well and were well led the next day, had taken the wrong road and would not arrive until after nightfall.

As night fell, the lead troops of Buell's army began pouring into Pittsburg Landing. General William "Bull" Nelson, who was broad and well over six feet tall, got off his ferry and became furious at the sight of over a thousand men at the landing, standing about, crying, laying down, or wandering about senseless—these were the men who had begun running from the field earlier in the day and who were joined by others throughout the battle. Nelson was absolutely mad with anger and waded into the crowd of men, striking some of them with the flat of his sword and threatening to begin shooting them. He even ordered his personal escort to draw sabers and "trample these bastards into the mud!" As this was happening, another Union unit was brought across the river, and as they attempted to disembark, they were stormed by the panicked men on the shore, whom they had to fight off with rifle butts. These men (units from Ohio and Illinois) actually made it to the front lines at Owl Creek, and their cannons helped to fight off the Confederate assaults there.

For his part, General Nelson sent a messenger to Grant, asking him for permission to begin shooting deserters. A call from General Grant to see him at his headquarters and the pleas of his aides calmed General Nelson down.

U. S. Grant had had a close call earlier in the day. As he was riding behind the lines to get an idea of the situation, a nearby aide had his head blown off by a shell. A splinter from that shell hit and cracked Grant's sword scabbard. Now, at about 6 p.m., Grant wondered whether or not General Buell meant to send more than just Nelson's troops across the river. He stood above Pittsburg Landing near his headquarters and pondered the situation. An aide approached him and waited for orders from Grant, who was talking to himself. The aide overheard him say, "Not beaten yet by a damn sight."

Grant didn't need to worry. All through the night, Buell's men came over the Tennessee River and set up camp near Grant's headquarters. At one point, however, some of his officers began wondering whether or not they would be better moving east across the river themselves and fighting another day. One of these was Sherman, who voiced doubts about the situation to other officers, but when he approached Grant at about 9 p.m., finding him quite a few yards from his headquarters, standing under a tree in the rain, he said nothing except to state the obvious. "Well, Grant, we've had the devil's own day, haven't we?" Grant barely looked up and said, "Yes. Whip them tomorrow though." Sherman dismissed all ideas about moving to the far side of the river after that.

Illustration 28: Site of Grant's tree today. Courtesy Matthew Gaskill.

Grant had taken his place under the oak because his headquarters and the area around it were full of wounded men, their limbs being sawed off by surgeons. The screaming and cries were more than Grant could take, and he had wandered off to be alone with his thoughts. Before Sherman came up, he had tried to get out of the rain and went back to his headquarters, but the screams of the wounded were just too much for him, so he returned to his place under the tree, lantern in one hand, cigar in his mouth.

That night, a thunderstorm struck the Shiloh area. Under the glare of lightning, troops saw and heard horrific things. One of those men was Confederate soldier Henry Morton Stanley, who was a Welsh immigrant in the 6th Arkansas Brigade. He had been captured toward the end of the day. As he sat with his fellow prisoners, he, like many others that night, listened to the moans and screams of the wounded in the field, and worse, he saw wild hogs feeding on the dead and nearly dead. Stanley would free himself from captivity by volunteering to join the Union Army, but he was discharged after suffering a serious illness. He then joined the Union Navy and served on board the USS *Minnesota* as a clerk. If his name sounds familiar, it's because he went on to become a world-famous explorer and found the lost Dr. Henry Livingstone, who had disappeared in his search for the Nile. Stanley's (supposed) famous line was "Dr. Livingstone, I presume?"

On the Confederate side, a sequence of serious mistakes were made. First was Beauregard's ill-timed telegraph to Jefferson Davis claiming "total victory." Next, many of the tired officers and men of the Confederacy simply dropped where they were or were ordered to move back to the rear, with some, namely Polk's men, going back near their starting point that morning. Worse, no real effort was made to organize the scattered men and units to prepare for a possible Union attack the next day, and no additional ammunition was brought forward, at least not to most of the units.

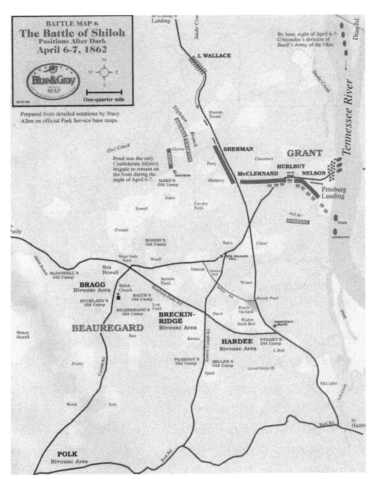

Illustration 29: The positions of both armies at the end of the day.
Courtesy Blue & Gray Magazine.

Conclusion

By the next day, April 7th, Ulysses S. Grant had forty thousand men at his disposal. Half of these men were fresh. Most of them were from Buell, the bulk of whose forces had made it across the river during the night. Just shortly after sundown, Lew Wallace's troops arrived after their unintended detour and were put into the line.

Against the Union's forty thousand men were about twenty-eight thousand Rebel troops, virtually all of whom were exhausted and ill-prepared for the Union counterattack, which began at about 6 a.m. For about two hours, the Rebels held the Yankees and even mounted two surprisingly savage counterattacks in the mid-morning, but the Union forces were too much for them. By about two in the afternoon, they had been pushed back past their original starting point, and Beauregard ordered them to fall back to Corinth. Grant's men did not pursue them until the next day, allowing the Southerners to escape to Corinth, which was besieged from April 29th to the 30th, finally falling into Union hands.

Over twenty-four thousand men were killed, wounded, or went missing at Shiloh, the worst toll of the Civil War up to that time. And despite the bloodshed at Gettysburg, Petersburg, and the other places fought in the South, the Battle of Shiloh still remained in the top ten of the war's bloodiest battles.

Shiloh showed the nation that the war was going to take much, much longer and be much bloodier than had ever been imagined. Immediately after the battle, many people in the North criticized Grant for the slaughter at Shiloh. Many in Washington pressured Lincoln to dismiss him, but the president replied, "I can't spare this man; he fights!" Of course, Grant went on to command all the Union forces from the beginning of 1864 to the war's end, and he also became the eighteenth president of the United States.

Both sides made glaring errors at Shiloh. The men of the South underestimated Grant's willingness to fight, they lacked discipline in their march toward the battle, Johnston should never have gone to the front as he did, and, most of all, the officers of the Confederacy let their men down by not reorganizing and resupplying their men at the end of the first day.

On the Union side, the overconfidence of Grant, Sherman, and others caused them to be surprised by the Rebel attack on April 6th. Had they dug in, perhaps more men would have lived, and the battle might have ended much sooner. The lack of Grant's, Wallace's, and Nelson's urgency in reinforcing Pittsburg Landing also cost lives. Still, the Battle of Shiloh was another Union victory, and it was especially important to them since the men in blue were being defeated time after time in Virginia and Maryland.

Here's another book by Captivating History that you might like

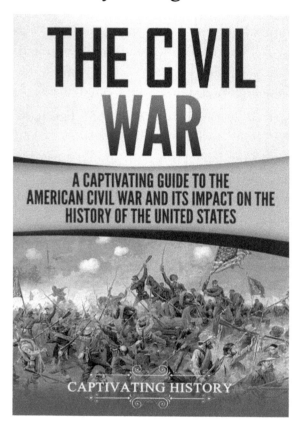

Free Bonus from Captivating History (Available for a Limited time)

Hi History Lovers!

Now you have a chance to join our exclusive history list so you can get your first history ebook for free as well as discounts and a potential to get more history books for free! Simply visit the link below to join.

Captivatinghistory.com/ebook

Also, make sure to follow us on Facebook, Twitter and Youtube by searching for Captivating History.

Bibliography

"Account of the Battle of Shiloh." HistoryNet. Last modified June 12, 2006. https://www.historynet.com/account-of-battle-of-shiloh.htm.

Allen, Stacy D. "Shiloh." BLUE & GRAY MAGAZINE, 2018.

"The Battle of Shiloh in Quotes." The Historians Manifesto. Last modified September 6, 2012. https://thehistoriansmanifesto.wordpress.com/2012/09/06/the-battle-of-shiloh-in-quotes/.

Catton, Bruce, and James M. McPherson. AMERICAN HERITAGE HISTORY OF THE CIVIL WAR. New Word City, 2014.

Daniel, Larry J. SHILOH: THE BATTLE THAT CHANGED THE CIVIL WAR. New York: Simon & Schuster, 2008.

"Digital History." UH - Digital History. Accessed May 25, 2021. https://www.digitalhistory.uh.edu/disp_textbook.cfm?smtID=3&psid=403.

Foote, Shelby. THE CIVIL WAR: A NARRATIVE. FORT SUMTER TO PERRYVILLE. New York: Vintage, 1986.

McPherson, James M., BATTLE CRY OF FREEDOM: THE CIVIL WAR ERA. New York: Oxford University Press, 1988.

Nevin, David. THE ROAD TO SHILOH: EARLY BATTLES IN THE WEST. Morristown, NJ: Time-Life, 1983.

"Our Wish for a Hard Battle A Chicago Artilleryman's Account of the Battle of Shiloh." Illinois Periodicals Online at Northern Illinois University - (Main Page). Accessed May 25, 2021. https://www.lib.niu.edu/1998/ihwt9827.html.

Southern veterans giving the Rebel yell: https://www.youtube.com/watch?v=s6jSqt39vFM&ab_channel=Smith sonianMagazine.

"Shiloh: Primary Sources." Spartacus Educational. Accessed May 25, 2021. https://spartacus-educational.com/USACWshiloh.htm.
(Despite its political leanings, this website has some extraordinary primary documents and accounts available.)

"A Soldier's Story: Battle of Shiloh." Belle on the Battlefield. Last modified January 27, 2019. https://belleonthebattlefield.wordpress.com/2019/01/30/a-soldiers-story-battle-of-shiloh/.

CPSIA information can be obtained
at www.ICGtesting.com
Printed in the USA
BVHW010332050822
643867BV00002B/10